On the
British
Narrow
Gauge

Previous page: Back in July 1959, Isle of Man Railway 2-4-0T No 16 *Mannin* takes the 10.35 Port Erin-Douglas past a slotted post signal (still extant in 1979) south of Castletown./*Frank Church*

Below: On the occasion of a railway society visit of 12 August 1968, Bowaters' 0-4-2ST *Premier* shunts at Sittingbourne./*R. A. Cover*

On the
British
Narrow
Gauge

Michael Harris

LONDON

IAN ALLAN LTD

First published 1980

ISBN 0 7110 0960 0

Published by Ian Allan Ltd, Shepperton, Surrey,
and printed by Ian Allan Printing Ltd
at their works
at Coombelands in Runnymede, England.

For Edmund

Below: Two months after the transfer of the old
Festiniog Railway Company to its new owners;
trespassers are warned at Boston Lodge Works in
August 1954./H. C. Casserley

Right: Driver's view from a Vale of Rheidol 2-6-2T
during July 1971./R. H. Dyer

Contents

Acknowledgements
In preparing this photographic review of the British narrow gauge I was greatly assisted by photographers who kindly and willingly presented me with a wide choice of their work. I would like to record my grateful thanks to David Eatwell, John Edgington, Norman Gurley, H. C. Casserley and Brian Morrison. Apart from giving me permission to use some of his prints, Mr A. B. MacLeod greatly assisted my efforts by offering useful advice and taking great trouble to unearth references, as have my other colleagues at Ian Allan Ltd.

The narrow gauge~setting the scene

The standard gauge railway seemed much more appealing. There were larger, more varied types of locomotives, the glamour of main line expresses and a more obvious scheme of things. Narrow gauge railways, almost entirely defunct in the late 1950s, seemed unglamorous, with model-like locomotives of too individualistic characters. Don't forget that over 20 years ago the attraction to many (and certainly to me) was that the Great Western or Southern atmosphere and practice were ubiquitous in their own territory and 'company' loyalties, even at that late hour of steam, remained strong. But none of the narrow gauge lines seemed to qualify as 'proper' railways; they appeared much too local and fragmented.

Holidays near the erstwhile Lynton & Barnstaple began my education. There was the poignancy of the surviving landmarks and then, only a generation after its closure, the grass was thinner in the cuttings than it is today. Memories were not dimmed either and the elderly were wont to murmur about the line in the dreaded Southern National route 110 buses. Before long I had travelled on the narrow gauge and had been thoroughly converted.

The point of relating these commonplaces is this: to many interested in railways the narrow gauge, other than as a preserved or tourist operation, is an anachronism. It is also a thing of the more distant past than 'Black Fives' on Shap or 'Castles' at Paddington; it is ancient history. Nor have many of the books on narrow gauge railways helped by presenting a picture of a past golden age

Right: Narrow gauge character — the Welshpool & Llanfair Light Railway at Castle Caereinion during 1977. A westbound train approaches with 0-6-0T No 1 *The Earl,* **original motive power for the line.** */M. Dunnett*

7

contrasted with the 'unreality' of today's survivors. In fact, the narrow gauge has never really died: even after the Festiniog had closed in 1946 the industrial lines, the Talyllyn and the Vale of Rheidol were still very much alive. By the mid/late 1960s, the more notable industrial lines may have succumbed to road transport, conveyors, or some less usual fate, but the narrow gauge phoenix had risen again.

For the principle of narrow gauge has always been that the smaller trackbed required, the sharper curve radii and tolerance of less well engineered earthworks enable this type of railway to exploit opportunities denied to 4ft 8½in gauge and what may be called traditional railway operation. Although it is romantic to think of the narrow gauge serving a rural community, or moving slate or ironstone, it is surely just as acceptable that it should carry sightseers or holidaymakers. Indeed, this is just what the Vale of Rheidol or Snowdon Mountain Railways always have done. Somehow, though, the present-day characteristic of the narrow gauge as an entertainment tends to be frowned on by the initiated, despite the fact that this mode of transport has merely adapted to what it is more efficient at doing.

Compared to horse and cart, the steam narrow gauge freight railway was more efficient but against modern conveyors or dumper trucks it had to give way. But to cater for an age of increased leisure by providing a mode of transport sufficient in both capacity and interest, what better than a narrow gauge steam railway to move visitors around pleasure gardens or an estate, or through fine country? Not surprisingly, several examples of the pleasure gardens and stately home genre have been added to the narrow gauge scene during the 1970s. As an aside, it is pleasant to reflect on the reported remark of the creator of the delectable Portmeirion, the late Sir Clough Williams-Ellis, to the effect that he liked the idea of an offshoot from the Festiniog serving the village. If executed, this would no doubt have provided an entertainment and transport facility of the highest kind. No matter that many of today's narrow gauge railways are selling 'trips' or entertainment, rather than being conventional providers of transport, nor that they are not public railways in the strictest sense. The important thing is that the narrow gauge concept and its artefacts be put to good use.

What are the particular characteristics of narrow gauge? Not the mechanical or civil engineering details in themselves, but the essential atmosphere that is derived from them. It is all a question of scale. Standard gauge permanent way, and certainly in its modern form with continuously welded rail and deep ballasting, is remorseless at ground level. But a single narrow gauge line (often with those slight irregularities of the sort that make life in general interesting) is to a much happier scale for the lineside walker. As modern railways necessarily become even more mechanistic and less related to their immediate locality, we shall treasure those lines whose every twist and turn reveals something new. What is more, the narrow gauge is inherently suited to causing the minimum disturbance to its environment, and thereby keeping to a modest scale. Where better to see this than on the Welshpool & Llanfair, or the Talyllyn, where the gentle and subtle beauty of the respective localities is best appreciated from the appropriately sized trains. And, of course, all the civil engineering works and structures are correspondingly scaled. The buildings and station areas are less like industrial development and more akin to some rural trades. With the Festiniog's Deviation route above Dduallt, the British narrow gauge enters the heroic scale, but in the locality's rocky and open country the railway seems to have struck a fine balance between establishing a presence and keeping in character.

Another aspect is by definition more fleeting. In a pleasant evocation of a last trip to the Welshpool & Llanfair (*Trains Illustrated,* December 1956), the late Dr Tuplin identified this characteristic precisely. As he approached Welshpool he noticed that apart from the normal (standard gauge) locomotive smoke there 'drifted a smoke-cloud of the lighter shade that seems peculiar to small engines when they have been fired just before the first run of the day'. That's exactly it! There is something fleeting about the combustion products of narrow (and miniature) gauge steam locomotives that is very different from the puissance of their larger brethren. Equally, Hamilton Ellis's charming reminiscence of the Lynton & Barnstaple (Waterloo-Lynton 1935, *Trains Illustrated,* May 1955) likens the progress of the train to a rabbit 'scuttling' and observes that the train, being relatively near to the ground, appeared to be travelling faster than it actually was. Ten years later, experiencing what proved to be the last few weeks of the old Isle of Man Railway's operation as a public carrier, those descriptions came back to

Welsh narrow gauge at the beginning of the 1950s:
(above) in the last season before the preservation
society took over, Talyllyn 0-4-0WT No 2 *Dolgoch* on
an afternoon train at Towyn (now Tywyn) Wharf on
11 August 1950. (below) Resuscitation of the
Festiniog, although mooted, had yet to come. This is
Blaenau Ffestiniog with the ex-LNWR station (left)
and the FR station (foreground). With the general
closure of the FR in 1946, the Maenofferen and Votty
quarries leased 650yd of the railway connecting their
quarry inclines with the LMS and GWR yards as an
outlet for their traffic; this section was still used by
trains when photographed in August 1951./D. Trevor
Rowe; R. H. G. Simpson

Above: Narrow gauge summer: in June 1978 Vale of Rheidol 2-6-2T No 7 *Owain Glyndwr* **(oil-fired) climbs to Devil's Bridge with the 10.15 from Aberystwyth.** */Brian Morrison*

me. Morose though the crew might be, they ran their train smartly, and the way in which it sprang away from each station and rocketed along the track recalled Hamilton Ellis's description of the L&B train.

The charm of the narrow gauge also derives from the dimension of the locomotives and rolling stock. Impressive though it is to be overawed by the six-foot driving wheels of a main line locomotive when standing at track level, the contrast of being able to come to terms with the more manageable proportions of a narrow or miniature machine is refreshing. Not that smallness makes for a lack of audible effort. The last mile up to Devil's Bridge on a (typically) damp and drizzly Welsh day bears comparison with any main line steam action to be found today. Similarly puissant sounds can be listened to on the miniature gauge, as when a Romney, Hythe & Dymchurch Pacific or Mountain is opened up through, say, New Romney

station when working a through empty stock train.

Finally, the miniature gauge. It has always seemed an irony that our two leading lines, the Ravenglass and the Romney, Hythe & Dymchurch, should have developed in such contrasting tracts of country: one in the flatness of the Kentish marshlands and shingle; the other in the very different scale of the Lakeland hills. Each in its own way has served to display multum in parvo to its best advantage, whether in weaving through the woods of Eskdale or when running the last lap into Hythe station. In recent years there has effectively been an intermediate stage above the miniature lines on those new narrow gauge systems where former small industrial locomotives, now domiciled in estates and gardens, evoke the spirit, if not perhaps the atmosphere, of the original Heywood and Sand Hutton lines, as they chug their way through shrubberies and edge past well-manicured lawns. Miniature 'estates and gardens' and the more historic narrow gauge — in each case they operate in a very different dimension and atmosphere to the 4ft 8½in gauge standard and provide a fascinating and refreshing contrast.

Above: Miniature gauge summer: heavily loaded
trains cross on the Ravenglass & Eskdale at Irton
Road in August 1975. Foreground – 2-8-2 *River Esk* of
1923 bound for Ravenglass awaits the 1966 vintage
River Mite en route for Dalegarth./*R. E. B. Siviter*

Below: 'Stately home' narrow gauge summer: a
steam roundabout at Bressingham Hall gardens is
passed by ex-Penrhyn Quarries 0-4-0ST *Gwynedd*
(built Hunslet, 1883) operating on the 1ft 11½in line
in July 1971./*David Eatwell*

Above: The gentle valley traversed by the Welshpool & Llanfair, near Castle Caereinion – a standard wartime German 0-8-0T acquired from Austria, now No 10 *Sir Drefaldwyn,* heads ex-British Naval and Austrian (second coach) stock in 1975./*M. Dunnett*

Top right: The equally verdant backcloth for the Talyllyn, although overshadowed by mountains, is seen on a damp September morning of low cloud in 1968 with the train headed for Abergynolwyn (then the terminus)./*M. Dunnett*

Right: The narrow gauge right of way seldom intrudes. Whereas the upgraded road from Maentwrog to Blaenau cuts unfeelingly through the countryside, the Festiniog, despite its 400,000 passenger journeys a year, hardly detracts from the scenery. *Merddin Emrys* at Campbell's Curve, below Dduallt, with the 15.30 Dduallt – Porthmadog on 29 May 1978./*John Scrace*

Left: Llanberis boasts the 2ft 7½in gauge Snowdon Mountain Railway, the 1ft 11½in gauge Llanberis Lake Railway (Rheilffordd Llyn Llanberis), and the excellent Dinorwic Slate Quarries Museum. (top left) Business seems brisk at the Llanberis (Gilfach Ddu) terminus of the Llanberis Lake Railway in late May 1978, with a Penllyn train behind No1 *Elidir,* a Hunslet 0-4-0ST, and (right) No 3 *Dolbadarn,* another Hunslet 0-4-0ST, also ex-Dinorwic. (bottom left) Llanberis shed of the Snowdon Mountain Railway, with locomotives being prepared in early June 1978. All are products of the Swiss Locomotive Company: No 7 *Aylwin* (of 1923), No 5 *Moel Siabod* (of 1896) and No 3 *Wyddfa* (of 1895)./*Both: Brian Morrison*

Right: Looking out from the Talyllyn Railway's Towyn Pendre shed on 1 June 1932. In the background is 0-4-0WT *Dolgoch,* while the passenger stock consists of two 1866/7 coaches and the guard's brake and luggage van./*H. C. Casserley*

Below: Ravenglass shed on 31 July 1968 with *River Mite* taking things easily./*T. J. Edgington*

Right: Miniature railway scale: New Romney station of the Romney Hythe & Dymchurch Railway in August 1976. Prospective passengers admire 1927-built 4-8-2 No 6 *Samson* at the head of a Hythe train while a four-wheel petrol locomotive waits behind.
/*Brian Morrison*

Below: Narrow gauge scale: an Isle of Man Railway Douglas-Ramsey train (line now closed) scoots along the cliffs north of St Germains in July 1959.
/*Frank Church*

The end of the line

So many summaries have been penned on the demise of the conventional narrow gauge that it is tempting to believe that photographs will say it all. The narrow gauge died in mainland Britain (and in Ireland) because it had always been economically and practically marginal. Of course, it was killed by motor competition, but having made the initial, and usually unprofitable, initial investment the various railways were steadily disinvested and run down. Apart from the Southern Railway's genuine attempt to bring the Lynton & Barnstaple up to acceptable standards after the 1923 Grouping, and the Great Western Railway's re-equipment of the Vale of Rheidol to perform a specialised task, the remainder of conventional narrow gauge lines were steadily worked to a standstill. It was then a question of the process of rundown being matched by, or overtaken by, the development of rural road

Below: Similar views of the Festiniog's Boston Lodge Works between 1946 and 1954 have appeared before, but little else pinpoints the nadir of the Railway's fortunes so well. Left is the single-bogie Fairlie 0-6-4T No 11 *Moel Tryfan,* scrapped in 1954. Behind Double Fairlie No 10 *Merddin Emrys* (in use today) is 0-4-0ST *Prince* (returned to traffic in 1979). This was the scene in March 1951./*H. C. Casserley*

transport making use of cheap vehicles which proved so efficient during World War I.

Further, many of the undertakings and extraction industries (slate, coal, clay, public utilities) served by narrow gauge lines were marginal, or being worked out, or loath to modernise. In these cases, and particularly with the industrial lines, narrow gauge transport had started out as the best solution to move often awkward traffic. But some time was to elapse before efficient road motor vehicles were produced to provide a better, if less picturesque, alternative. Although the general-purpose motor lorry, often War Surplus, was quickly available after 1918, the precursor of the modern dump truck took longer to come into the picture. Unless distances were short, conveyor systems were not very efficient. The slate industry quarries were usually far enough from shipping for their narrow gauge feeders to linger on, while the quarry companies, if they owned the railways, were hardly encouraged to spend money on new transport facilities, the industry having been weakened by the great Penrhyn strike of 1900-3 and the loss of export markets in the two world wars. A visit to the Dinorwic Slate Quarries quarry maintenance workshops at Llanberis, so fortunately and successfully preserved by the National Museum of Wales, demonstrates very clearly that much of the slate industry had become obsolete long before its demise in the postwar period. Thus the continuation of narrow gauge rail facilities was not an anachronism when the slate quarries themselves had become museum pieces of Victorian industry.

Otherwise, the remaining lines (Southwold, Leek & Manifold, Lynton & Barnstaple and Welsh Highland) were all subject to the same defects. Whether or not they had become a possession of one of the Big Four after Grouping, they were subject to the difficulties of transhipment. While we might marvel at the survival of some standard gauge branch lines through the economic tribulations of the 1930s, faced as they were with road competition, they were nonetheless all part of a large network. Only with the advent of Dr Beeching did railway management start to isolate the costs of running individual stretches of railway. Until that time so long as the main line railways provided a common carrier service throughout their territories, the carriage of household coal and basic goods traffic made nearly all their system worth keeping. But the isolated, narrow gauge lines (nor-

mally short in length in any case) involved transhipment, and the sheer inconvenience for small amounts of traffic was obvious, as were the costs of maintaining a specialised stretch of railway. So the decisions of the SR and LMS to shut up shop on the Lynton & Barnstaple and the Leek & Manifold were clearly determined. Only the GWR had the foresight to develop the Vale of Rheidol to handle the traffic to which it was best suited, but then it had been constructed to cater for tourist traffic in the first place.

Fortunately, human activity seldom submits to wide generalisations and a fascinating variety of narrow gauge activity survived into the postwar era. Many industrial systems (East Midlands ironstone, Thames-side paper mills, Purbeck clay) were just specialised enough, or else interwoven with production processes, to survive into the 1950s and 1960s so that the enthusiasts and preservationists could marvel at their equipment, ride on them or pick up the pieces for posterity. Many such works systems were remarkable examples of industrial archaeology. Even then sand and gravel quarries still found use for narrow gauge railways into the 1970s, until conveyors or dump trucks struck the final blow and remnants such as British Industrial Sands' Legiate system in Norfolk passed into history at the end of the 1970s. All told, from horsepower through picturesque steam traction and on to internal combustion tractors, narrow gauge railways probably had a better innings than may appear at first sight. Faced with such diversity on the mainland, and not forgetting the Isle of Man Railways, to attempt to cover the Irish narrow gauge would overload the applecart. For this reason, in *The Lines that Died* (and in this study as a whole), we go no further across the Irish Sea than Port Erin or Peel.

Centre left: The 2ft 6in gauge Pentewan Railway which connected the port of Pentewan with St Austell in Cornwall was principally a china clay transporter and finally closed in 1918. This is the 1901 vintage Manning Wardle 0-6-2ST *Canopus* toying with a china clay wagon near the Pentewan road crossing alongside the Winnick River. */LPC*

Bottom left: The Southwold Railway, of 3ft gauge, was opened 100 years ago and has been closed for 50. No 3 *Blyth*, a Sharp Stewart 2-4-0T, seen at Southwold./*LPC*

19

Above: Travelling by narrow gauge – the view out through the verandah of a Campbeltown and Macrihanish Railway coach; this 2ft 3in gauge line in Kintyre died in 1931. The view dates from 2 August 1930./H. C. Casserley

Centre right: The Campbeltown & Macrihanish connected with the tourist steamers but coal was the staple traffic. This is 1906-built *Argyll* at the Hall Street terminus, Campbeltown, in May 1928, waiting with a mixed train./H. C. Casserley Collection

Bottom right: The LMS inherited the Leek & Manifold Valley from Waterhouses to Hulme End in Staffordshire. A train for Hulme End approaches Thor's Cave Halt on 29 April 1933, less than a year before closure./H. C. Casserley

20

Above: The Leek & Manifold was interesting for its use of transporter wagons. For a short period up to 1932 Ecton creamery loaded standard gauge milk tanks consigned to Finsbury Park, but the creamery was destined to close. Two transporters are behind No 1 *E. R. Calthorp./Rixon Bucknall Collection, Ian Allan Library*

Below: The dismal scene on the Leek & Manifold as a grimy *E. R. Calthorp* is employed in the demolition of its own line during April 1937, here paused at Redhurst Crossing. The locomotive was cut up at Waterhouses in October 1937./*H. C. Casserley Collection*

Top left: Narrow gauge railways tended to appear in family photo albums. This is a typical instance which shows the 1ft 11½in gauge Lynton & Barnstaple, under SR control, of course, in the summer of 1934. At Lynton station is 2-6-2T No 759 *Yeo* with third-class observation coach SR No 2468./*B. R. Robinson*

Left: We shall probably never again see regular mixed narrow gauge trains. This is Lynton in 1935 with stock standing in the station./*A. B. MacLeod*

Above: Outside the summer peak the fortunes of the Lynton & Barnstaple line were different. No 761 *Taw* gathers speed having left Barnstaple Town and passes the Town Mill with a mixed train in the winter of 1935./*Donovan E. H. Box*

Left: *Lew* stands at Chelfham in 1935 with a Barnstaple bound train. The viaduct can be seen beyond and a down train is signalled. Note the catchpoint in the siding./*A. B. MacLeod*

Below left: The 2-6-2T supplied to the Lynton & Barnstaple section by the Southern Railway after Grouping, No 188 *Lew,* takes water at Pilton in 1935./*A. B. MacLeod*

Below: The narrow gauge will be remembered as long as there are monuments such as Chelfham Viaduct of the Lynton & Barnstaple, 70ft in height. It is now a protected structure./*J. T. Palm*

Above: After World War I some narrow gauge concerns purchased War Surplus locomotives to bolster up ageing motive power studs, for example this Baldwin 4-6-0PT (No 45221 of 1917) which after an expensive overhaul went to the Glyn Valley Tramway in 1921./*LPC*

Top right: The Glyn Valley Tramway (2ft 4½in gauge) relied on several sources of freight traffic, but ironically it was a fall in demand for roadstone granite chippings that led to its demise in 1935. This is Glynceiriog coal yard – coal merchant's office (left), water tower (right)./*LPC*

Right: By and large, the islands round Britain's coast have hung on to their railways fairly successfully. Not so the Channel Islands, and both railways in Jersey had gone by 1936. The Jersey Railway, originally standard gauge, was converted to 3ft 6in gauge and latterly depended on four Sentinel-Cammell railcars for its passenger workings. Here is No 1 *The Pioneer* (of 1923) at First Tower station in 1928./*Reginald F. Smith*

26

Above left: One of the most attractive narrow gauge steam locomotives was *Russell* (before being brutalised, that is) built for the North Wales Narrow Gauge Railways by Hunslet in 1910. Here it is at Beddgelert, shortly after opening of this section as the Welsh Highland Railway in 1923./*LPC*

Left: To gain access to Portmadoc Harbour station and the Festiniog, the Welsh Highland crossed the GWR's Pwllheli-Barmouth line, east of the GWR station. This is the crossing with the GWR with the WHR Portmadoc New station beyond./*LPC*

Above: Shortly after interworking between the Festiniog and Welsh Highland began, *Russell* was taken into Boston Lodge to be cut down to suit the FR's loading gauge, but to no avail. After the closure of the WHR *Russell* was sold for further use and eventually passed to B. Fayle & Co Ltd's clay railway, near Corfe Castle, Dorset. She is seen here at Corfe Castle clay works in July 1949./*Donovan E. H. Box*

Right: Demolition of the Welsh Highland in Aberglaslyn Pass on 13 August 1941./*A. E. Rimmer*

Above: The Saundersfoot Railway (4ft ⅜in gauge) was built to carry coal from the isolated Pembrokeshire coalfield in the early 1830s. It lasted until 1939, a good example of a 'marginal' railway serving an equally 'marginal' industry. This view shows the loading spouts for coastal vessels at Saundersfoot Harbour. Note the primitive coal drams./LPC

Below: Narrow gauge lines were often built to tap mineral resources beyond the reach of standard gauge branches, a typical example being the Snailbeach District Railways in Shropshire, promoted in the 1870s and built to 2ft 4in gauge. These are the exchange sidings at Pontesbury, c1925, with the standard gauge link from the GWR/LMS Joint Shrewsbury-Minsterley branch – right background. /LPC

Above: Surprisingly few British narrow gauge railways were built under the provisions of the 1896 Light Railway Act. The little 3ft gauge Rye & Camber Tramway was registered in the year before its passing and was not even built under an Act of Parliament. A holidaymaker's line pure and simple, it was perfectly suited to its task. This is the corrugated iron station at Rye, with the engine and carriage sheds in the background./*LPC*

Left: The Rye & Camber was extended to Camber Sands in 1908. This April 1931 photograph depicts the interwar atmosphere (the line died in 1939) — note the driver-conductor with yachting cap! The original passenger vehicle is paired with the rather basic petrol 'locomotive' of 1925./*H. C. Casserley*

Above: The 2ft 3in gauge Corris Railway unusually came to be purchased by the GWR in 1930 because the latter wanted its owning company's bus network. Sometime in the 1920s Kerr, Stuart-built 0-4-2ST No 4 (now on the Talyllyn) takes water at the main shed and works of the Corris at Maespoeth Junction. /LPC

Right: The Ashover Light Railway, near Clay Cross, Derbyshire, was a 2ft gauge line, built to tap limestone and fluorspar deposits. Opened to traffic in April 1925, it was the most recent narrow gauge line in Britain of any length, and for all types of traffic, but lasted only a generation. (top right) In the late 1920s one of the line's ex-Baldwin-built War Department 4-6-0PTs, *Hummy*, heads a passenger train. (bottom right) Now much more grimy and with a stovepipe chimney, *Hummy* stands at Clay Cross c1934./*Ian Allan Library; F. G. Carrier*

Above: The Dinorwic slate quarries output was shipped out through Port Dinorwic on the Menai Straits, being transported there by a seven-mile 4ft gauge line, the Padarn Railway, which stopped operations in October 1961. Four 1ft 10¾in quarry wagons were loaded on to each 4ft gauge transporter wagon, as shown in this June 1956 picture of one of the line's Hunslet 0-6-0Ts with a train nearing Port Dinorwic./R. E. Vincent

Top right: As described on page 9, the slate quarries at Blaenau Ffestiniog continued to despatch their products over part of the Festiniog Railway after the main line had closed. A view of May 1949 showing the inclines connecting Duffws station with the slate quarries, with abandoned FR rolling stock (left)./D. P. N. Callender

Right: Movements of slate wagons continued after the principal routes had closed in other parts of Wales as well, such as these examples seen in 1954 on the horse-drawn tramway at Aberllefenni, formerly feeding the Corris Railway./Michael E. Ware

The diversity of industrial narrow gauge lines was fascinating. One particularly attractive system was that of the Metropolitan Water Board, of 2ft gauge and around 3½ miles in length, linking the Thames-side wharf at Hampton with pumping stations at Kempton Park and Sunbury. Opened in 1915 to take coal to various pumping works, it was closed and dismantled by 1947. The motive power (left) was provided by three attractive Kerr, Stuart 0-4-2Ts, one of which, *Sunbury,* poses outside the shed at Hampton. (above) From water it is but a short step to beer. The Oakhill Brewery Co Ltd's 2ft 6in gauge line built to carry stout down to the Somerset & Dorset line at Binegar, near Bath, must have been a gem. Opened c1903/4, it closed as early as 1921. This is *Oakhill,* a Peckett 0-4-0ST of 1904./*Both: LPC*
Below: Paper is another valuable commodity and we have already met Bowaters' 2ft 6in gauge railway built to convey paper, at Sittingbourne in Kent. Well-equipped workshops were a rarity on most narrow gauge lines but this is the scene at the Kemsley Mill shops as late as 22 September 1969 (a month before closure as an industrial railway), with *Alpha* (left), a Bagnall 0-6-2T of 1932 (now preserved on the railway) and *Superior,* a Kerr, Stuart 0-6-2T of 1920 (now at Whipsnade)./*John H. Bird*

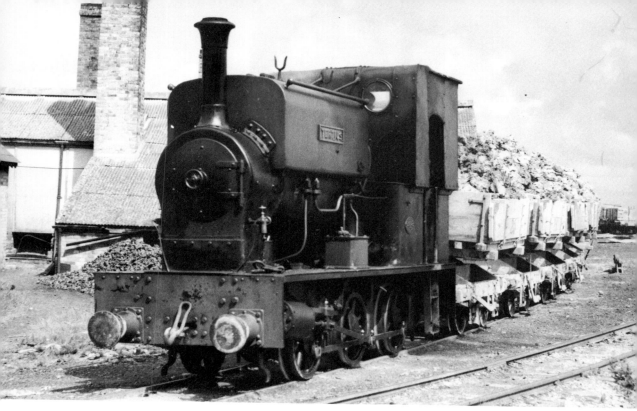

Clay kept narrow gauge lines busy, and both the 2ft 8in gauge Pike's Bros (Wareham) Ltd railway on the Isle of Purbeck and the Marland Light Railway on the borders of North Devon and Cornwall were concerned with ball clay. Opened in 1880, to 3ft gauge, part of the Marland Light Railway was later converted to standard gauge and is still in use. On the Furzebrook line (above), the unstable-looking Manning Wardle, *Tertius,* originally of 1886 but substantially rebuilt, heads a rake of typical wagons. The railway operated until 1957 and *Tertius* was scrapped two years later. (below) *Marland,* a Bagnall 0-6-0T of 1883, leaves Marland. Diesel-operated 3ft gauge clay trains ran on this line until 13 November 1970./*LPC*

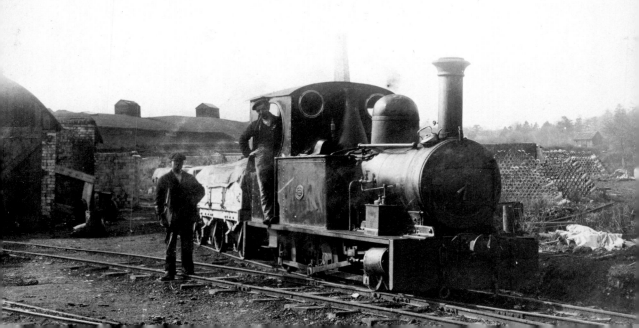

Elsewhere in Southern England chalk quarrying generated narrow gauge railways. At Betchworth (top) the Dorking Grey-Stone Lime Co Ltd roasted the chalk in kilns to produce lime from 1865. This is a view of the kilns from the middle level of the quarry, showing the 3ft 2¼in gauge line with one of the Fletcher, Jennings & Co 0-4-0Ts of 1880 – both of which were preserved with the closure of the system in 1960. (above) On the south bank of the Thames there were many lines connecting chalk quarries with cement works. One such was Swanscombe (White's) Cement Works, later controlled by the Associated Portland Cement Manufacturers Ltd, with a curious 3ft 5½in gauge line with flanges running *outside* the rails. Normal standard gauge track was installed in 1929, and some narrow gauge machines like *Hustler*, built Kilmarnock Engineering Co Ltd, 1920, lasted less than 10 years./*Both: LPC*

Above: Back to North Wales. It seems incredible that this scene is as recent as October 1961, when 1ft 10¾in gauge Dinorwic Slate Quarry Hunslet 0-4-0ST *Holy War* of 1902 was returning to her shed after a day's work. But she was used until November 1967, the last North Wales quarry steam locomotive in action. *Holy War* is now preserved on the Bala Lake Railway./*E. N. Kneale*

Right: Ironstone extraction also kept narrow gauge industrial steam lines in action until recent years. Until the early 1960s the traveller on a Midland main line express might catch a glimpse of a 3ft gauge Manning Wardle, just north of Kettering station. It was no doubt one of five locomotives of the Kettering Coal & Iron Co Ltd, such as *Kettering Furnaces* No 6 of 1889 (top right), heading a train of iron ore from the Rothwell quarry while sister engine No 7 (of 1897) waits to propel the wagons on to the tipping stage. Further south were Finedon Quarries with a metre gauge line which served an ironworks at Wellingborough (bottom right) On 19 September 1964 Peckett 0-6-0ST No 85 of 1934 (now preserved at Embsay) is cleaned and painted prior to a directors' inspection at its Finedon shed. By then this was the last narrow gauge line still operating in ironstone country and lasted until October 1966./*G. D. King; R. Fisher*

The narrow gauge phoenix

In *Railway Adventure* (David & Charles new editions 1961 et seq), the late L.T.C. Rolt described how a group of railway enthusiasts came to take over a railway, the Talyllyn Railway, thereby ushering in the era of railway preservation. Since January 1951 the Talyllyn Railway Preservation Society has maintained and administered the line, and a generation has now passed since railway enthusiasm was translated into the practicalities of a public facility. The Talyllyn is of course the line that *never closed* and the next project, the rescue and preservation of the Festiniog, involved dealing with a largely derelict railway. Since then a generation has passed since a skeleton service was first operated on part of the revivified Festioniog in July 1955.

It is easy to think that because both Talyllyn and Festiniog were threatened with extinction, so preservation was a reflex action. But the stalwarts involved with both rescues were practical (and enthusiastic) people who could see that despite the obvious problems the scale of the narrow gauge was such that the size of both rolling stock and equipment was manageable. Since then, railway preservation has steadily built on each new achievement so that the operation of 10-20 mile stretches of railway (North Yorkshire Moors and Severn Valley), the construction of a new railway (the Festiniog's Deviation) and the maintenance of main line standard gauge express locomotives which haul trains on BR metals all represent the current state of the art. Whereas the 19th century had seen narrow gauge railways develop after the pattern of the standard gauge example, railway preservation has seen 4ft 8½in practice take its cue from the smaller gauge.

Once the Talyllyn and Festiniog had established that the general public would pay — and in sufficient numbers, at that — to travel behind and in out-moded railway equipment — the narrow gauge phoenix had risen. Tourist railways have become part of the national economy. But the view that such railways sold 'trips' and not a transport service could be heard, especially in the late 1960s. Other detractors lamented (and still do) that in catering for increased traffic the preservation societies and railways were rapidly destroying that which they had set out to conserve. Both are wrong. 'Trips' in which the conveyance from 'A' to 'B' is entertainment, and not public transport, are just as valid a way of using a railway as in moving slate or workpeople. Narrow gauge railways were indeed built for tourists in the first place: the Vale of Rheidol was promoted as much to boost the area's tourist trade as to serve the local lead mines, while the Snowdon Mountain Railway and Snaefell have each never pretended to be anything other than a facility for tourists.

Except as a setpiece in a museum, a railway can never be preserved as some sort of moving tableau rooted in some frozen moment of past time. This is as artificial and unrealistic a view of transport as can be imagined. Today's Festiniog, with its oil-burning steam locomotives, new rolling stock, tourists' cafeteria and newly created stretch of line is self-evidently a far cry from an idea of the FR *as it was. As it was!* Who could seriously wish to recreate the sad decline of a once pioneering and noble railway in attempting to regain the imagined atmosphere of 1935, 1925 or even 1905? The pleasure, surely, is to see an efficient, popular and well maintained mode of transport building on the example and pattern of its earlier existence. Railway equipment, though extraordinarily long-lived, does wear out (even on static display), and as long as people want to see steam railways in action they must perforce accept the consequences. This is that to ensure the survival of the old, the railway must attract business in the most appealing way — within reason. Thus new Fairlies or all-steel rolling stock must be created, and track and signalling renewed if it is not to retreat into being a showcase of former, but unusable glories. Few could seriously argue otherwise.

One of the few examples of narrow gauge modernisation is the Vale of Rheidol, which was kept up to scratch by the Great Western Railway. This happened twice, in 1923 and again in the late 1930s. Yet no one would complain that the GWR's modernisation made the line uninteresting. Probably Paddington's general principle of keeping its railway network intact (and remembering that with its consistent, if modest, profits the GWR felt that it could afford to do so) ensured that the Vale of Rheidol survived, whereas the LMSR's Leek and Manifold and SR's Lynton & Barnstaple did not. Despite fairly consistent and regular maintenance in recent years, British Rail's attitude continues to be rather unimaginative and, at least, it would be nice to see the coaches painted in Inter-City livery.

Over on the Isle of Man, from 1978 the Manx Electric Railway, Isle of Man Steam Railway and Snaefell Mountain Railway have all come under the same state management. Some money has been spent on improvements and a more determined effort has been made to publicise the lines to the mainland market with the result that the traffic figures for 1979 showed dramatic increases over the previous year, and promise well for the future.

Below: Narrow gauge atmosphere at the Talyllyn's Pendre shed on a bright spring morning in 1977 as No 6 *Douglas* **is ready to start its day's work.**/M. Dunnett

The Talyllyn Railway (2ft 3in gauge) in the days before preservation. (above) *Dolgoch* (leading) and *Talyllyn* at Pendre in 1902. (right) *Talyllyn's* frames under repair at Pendre in June 1932. *Dolgoch* at work in June 1932: (below) above Abergynolwyn and proceeding up towards the quarries and (far right, top) beside the station with the guard's brake and luggage van at the front of the train. (far right, bottom) In 1945 the faithful *Dolgoch* was overhauled and repainted by Atlas Foundry, Shrewsbury, and this shows her in early postwar days at Abergynolwyn. */LPC; H. C. Casserley(three); E. Emrys Jones*

One wishes the managers well, particularly after the realisation that retrenchment in the shape of denying the steam railway a Douglas terminus and the closure of the Laxey-Ramsey section of the MER lost more in traffic receipts than was saved in reduced operating costs. Certainly, in the Isle of Man it has been learnt, if belatedly, that historic transport may be one reason for people visiting the island.

Finally, a word on the Welshpool & Llanfair, a line that survived as a traditional style public carrier as late as 31 October 1956. Today, with locomotives and rolling stock from three continents, and with continuous braking in place of loose coupled working, it provides a memorial of several lines now dead, of the narrow gauge railway quietly going about its business in a gentle and tranquil valley. Alongside, motor traffic (much of it providing the railway's custom) rushes past on the main road to the coast.

In each of the railways mentioned (and not forgetting the Snowdon Mountain Railway), the narrow gauge has adapted to what it can do best in the modern world. The phoenix has risen from the ashes to give one generation, if not more, an experience of another age.

Top left: Fastening the level crossing gates at Towyn Pendre during the first season of operation by the Talyllyn Railway Preservation Society, on 14 August 1951./R. H. G. Simpson

Left: The neat, ex-industrial railway four-wheel Ruston & Hornsby diesel of the TRPS, No 5 Midlander, contrasts with original TR passenger stock and slate wagons as it waits at a deserted Dolgoch station on 8 June 1957./M. E. Ware

Above: The TR of the early 1950s — with perhaps more than a little regret that this sort of atmosphere has gone. Dolgoch approaches Abergynolwyn with the last train from Towyn on 1 August 1953./D. R. Forsyth

47

Talyllyn in the mid-1960s: (top) The second
Abergynolwyn station (for the first see page 45) with
the refreshment van standing in the loop – the latter
an innovation of 1964. (above) From 1958-69 No 4
(ex-Corris) *Edward Thomas* sported a Giesl ejector and
waits at Tywyn Wharf with the 10.25 up on 7 June

1965, refreshment van next to the engine, followed
by the restored ex-Corris Rly coach. (right) A view of
the 52ft high Dolgoch viaduct is obligatory in any
review of the Talyllyn – here being traversed by No 6
in June 1966./*All: T. J. Edgington*

Left: Ex-Corris Railway 0-4-2ST, CR and TR No 3, now a centenarian, at Brynglas Crossing (above left) on an up train on 7 August 1973; and (bottom left) awaiting departure from Tywyn Wharf on 31 May 1969 – Corris coach next the engine./R. E. B. Siviter; David Eatwell

Above: 1864-built Talyllyn coasts into Abergynolwyn on 18 July 1975./T. J. Edgington

Right: The TR's extension beyond Abergynolwyn to Nant Gwernol was officially opened on 22 May 1976, work having started on site in the autumn of 1970. No 4 has arrived at the new terminus from Tywyn on 2 June 1978./Brian Morrison

Right: The 1ft 11½in gauge Festiniog Railway's Blaenau Ffestiniog Exchange (LNWR) station towards the close of the 19th century: 'Change here for Bettws-y-Coed & Llandudno'. The picture disguises the fact that there is a roadway between the stations. A George England 0-4-0 in the station. For a 1951 view, see page 9./*LPC*

Below: A turn of the century view at Minffordd (FR) with a Double Fairlie heading an up train of four wheelers – two 1870s bogie coaches and bogie brake./*LPC*

Bottom right: 0-4-0ST *Palmerston* poses, with crew, at Portmadoc Harbour station in the early 1900s./*LPC*

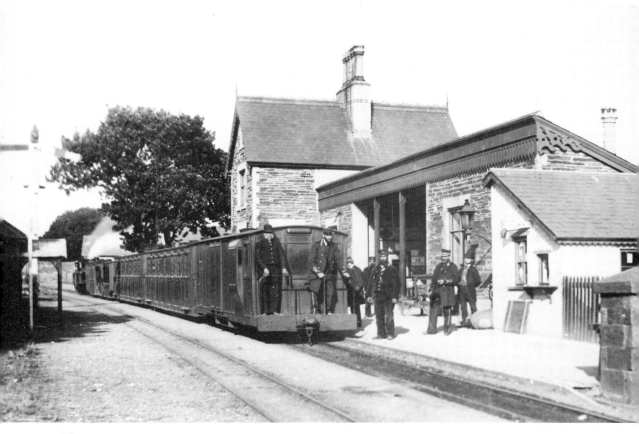

Above: A view from an up train in June 1932 hauled by a Double Fairlie crossing the 62ft stone embankment known as Cei Mawr./H. C. Casserley

Left: Twenty years later the FR was derelict, and Boston Lodge Works full of rotting equipment such as the two surviving 1923-built Robert Hudson 'toastracks'. A 1953 picture./M. E. Ware

Right: Before the 1950s were out, the Festiniog scene was altogether more hopeful. (top right) Two years after passenger trains had started running again, Prince rounds the curve past the entrance to Boston Lodge works on the 15.00 Portmadoc-Penrhyndeudraeth on 8 August 1957. (bottom right) By the next Easter the FR was back at Tan-y-Bwlch. Early in the 1959 season Double Fairlie Taliesin stands at Minffordd on an up train with vehicles in the then ivory and green livery. The leading coach is ex-Welsh Highland Railway. /R. E. Vincent; P. F. Winding

Left: Walking the dog at Minffordd in 1964. *Prince* sits patiently in the loop, awaiting the passage of a late running down train./*M. Dunnett*

Above: Double Fairlie No 10 *Merddin Emrys* leaves Portmadoc on 6 June 1963 with the 10.45 to Tan-y-Bwlch. The locomotive had returned to traffic two years earlier. Last but one coach is buffet car No 14,

newly in service that year, rebuilt from an ex-Lynton & Barnstaple coach, and the prototype for new FR coaches of the mid/late 1960s./*T. J. Edgington*

Below: An interesting line-up at Portmadoc Harbour in July 1964. (Left to right) the out of use 0-4-0ST *Princess*; ex-Penrhyn Railway Hunslet *Linda*; *Merddin Emrys* and *Prince*./*C. Lawson Kerr*

Right: An attractive shot of *Merddin Emrys* crossing the Cob at Porthmadog with the 15.15 bound for Dduallt on 27 May 1972./*J. Scrace*

Below: As in the above picture, the FR rolling stock was by now in its present red livery. *Merddin Emrys* again, this time at Coed Caefali with the 13.15 up train for Dduallt in August 1972. Next the engine is an ex-quarrymen's coach (now a brake) and two four-wheelers dating back to the 1860s./*J. Scrace*

Bottom right: By now an oil-burner, ex-Penrhyn Hunslet *Blanche* fitted with a leading truck approaches Minffordd in October 1973 with the 11.15 ex-Porthmadog. The first coach, No 116, is an all-metal vehicle, the prototype for new stock in the mid/late 1970s./*Brian Morrison*

Left: Ex-Penrhyn 2-4-0ST *Linda* sets out over the level crossing at Penrhyndeudraeth in August 1975. /M. Dunnett

Festiniog miscellany: (above) In July 1972, one of the last BR trains to enter the exchange sidings at Minffordd is propelled by a Class 24 diesel. The bogie bolsters are loaded with rail for the FR. (below left) The Matisa ballast tamper ingeniously converted from standard gauge in 1977. (below right) The renewal of pointwork at Tan-y-Bwlch in November 1973, assembled by the FR from 75lb/yd standard gauge rail seen arriving (top) at Minffordd./N. F. Gurley; FR Co (two)

Left: Any mention of the FR must feature the marvellous work of creating the 2¾ mile Deviation above Dduallt, a new stretch of railway and the biggest civil engineering project in railway preservation. Through services beyond Dduallt to Tan-y-Grisiau commenced in June 1978. Earlier, in December 1976 (top left), *Blanche* propels a train of sand round the spiral at Dduallt, necessary to gain height to reach the new line of route. In front of *Blanche* is ex-War Department Simplex diesel *Mary Ann.* (bottom left) The loading dock near Llyn Ystradau, midway on the new route, intended mainly for the transhipment of ballast and ready-mixed concrete but here (January 1977) used to receive slate waste used for trackbed formation. Note the tiny Lister works locomotive, named *Sludge./Both: N. F. Gurley*

Above: Finished result: the new route includes a section of *up* gradient facing down trains – unthinkable when loaded slate trains depended on gravity to reach Porthmadog. *Merddin Emrys* approaches the summit on the stretch (behind the lakeside power station) with a train from Tan-y-Grisiau on 9 July 1978./*R. Fisher*

63

Left: With 410,000 passenger journeys recorded in 1978, the FR is at the top of the private railway traffic league. Passengers stream off a charter train at Tan-y-Bwlch in June 1977, past *Merddin Emrys*.
/*N. F. Gurley*

Below left: FR diesel traction. In 1962 the Welshpool & Llanfair LR Preservation Co Ltd purchased a 1954-built four-wheeled diesel (later named *Upnor Castle*) from an Admiralty light railway. In 1968 it was sold to the FR and was suitably regauged and later re-engined; 10 years after in late May 1978 *Upnor Castle* stands in Porthmadog Harbour station with the 11.00 for Dduallt./*Brian Morrison*

Right: Shortly after trains regularly began running through to Tan-y-Grisiau, *Linda* runs forward to the headshunt at the new station (and faces towards Blaenau). At this point the Deviation rejoins the original line of route./*R. Fisher*

Below: Preserved railways operate outside the summer season, too, and Christmas-time Santa Specials are popular. Bedecked with fairy lights, *Merddin Emrys* prepares to leave the shed at Boston Lodge on 17 December 1977, ready to work the 14.15 ex-Porthmadog./*David Eatwell*

Above: Ex-War Department American-built locomotives played their part in the interwar British narrow gauge scene. Representing the breed is the Alco-built 2-6-2T of 1917, now *Mountaineer* on the FR, a locomotive imported in 1965 from the Tramway de Pithiviers à Toury and adapted to suit the FR. Shortly before services were extended to Tan-y-Grisiau, *Mountaineer* leaves Dduallt for Porthmadog in May 1978./*Brian Morrison*

Top right: The Vale of Rheidol, another 1ft 11½in gauge line, was opened towards the end of 1902 by an independent company, was purchased by the Cambrian Railways in 1903 and thence passed to the GWR. This is Devil's Bridge in Edwardian days. The locomotive on the left is Bagnall 2-4-0T No 3 *Rheidol*, the other is one of the 2-6-2Ts./*LPC*

Right: Front end view of one of two original Vale of Rheidol Railway 2-6-2Ts./*LPC*

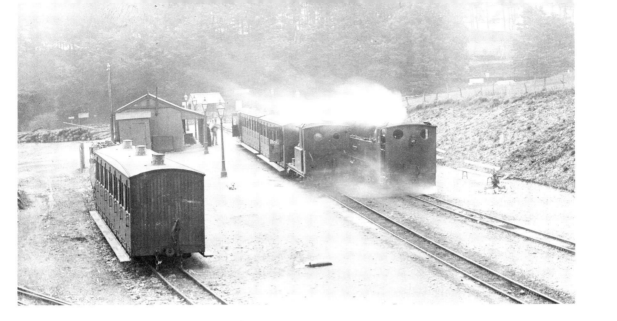

Top left: The former Aberystwyth station of the Vale of Rheidol (with the standard gauge station behind) which served until the end of the 1967 season. This is the terminus in early BR days, with the locomotives and stock still in GWR livery. Left is No 8 (of 1923), right is No 1213 (now No 9), one of the 1902 locomotives./H. C. Casserley

Left: In the days of the independent terminus, V of R No 9 *Prince of Wales* eases past the Crosville bus garage (and a Bristol K-type) into the station area with the 16.10 from Devil's Bridge on 4 June 1963. /*T. J. Edgington*

Above: It will be misty and wet up at Devil's Bridge! No 7 *Owain Glyndwr* takes a train of 1923 (open, tarpaulined) and 1938 (closed) coaches past Llanbadarn on 13 August 1958./*Brian Morrison*

69

Above: The former narrow/standard gauge transhipment siding outside Aberystwyth, in June 1963./T. J. Edgington

Left: The ground frame for the new Vale of Rheidol layout at Aberystwyth station, seen in late 1969. /G. M. Kichenside

Above right: Platform edge view of No 7 and its train at Aberystwyth in June 1978, five minutes away from leaving with the 14.15 to Devil's Bridge. Passengers load the other side./Brian Morrison

Right: Prince of Wales makes a smoky exit from Aberystwyth on 8 August 1977. Left background is the old coaling stage at the ex-GWR shed, right are the standard gauge lines./Peter Groom

Top left: Heavy work from No 9 making the final approach to Devil's Bridge with the 14.15 ex-Aberystwyth in July 1970. Note that No 9 is carrying a headlight, used when working the evening trains operated at that time./T. J. Edgington

Left: Blower on and taking water, No 8 Llywelyn is prepared for the climb up to Devil's Bridge at Aberffrwd on 28 July 1969 with the 14.15 ex-Aberystwyth./T. J. Edgington

Above: Spring comes late to the hillsides as on Good Friday 1977, No 7 (in its last season as a coal burner) storms up towards Devil's Bridge with the 13.30 ex-Aberystwyth./David Eatwell

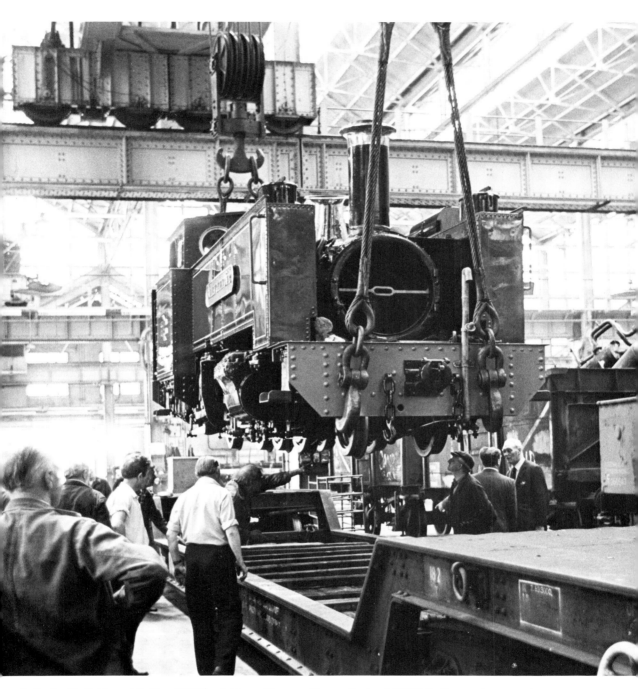

Left: Devil's Bridge on 3 June 1978 (compare with the photograph on page 67) with shop *and* buffet (the latter an innovation in that year). The noon departure for Aberystwyth with No 7./*Brian Morrison*

Above: During 1975/6 No 7 was given a major overhaul at BREL Swindon Works and was repainted in lined blue livery. She is seen here at the Works being lowered on to a transporter wagon./*R. C. H. Nash*

The Snowdon Mountain Railway is Britain's one and only rack railway and features the Abt rackrail and 2ft 7½in track gauge (80cm). After a disastrous opening in 1896, the line closed, reopening in August 1897 and continuing successfully and uneventfully through each successive season. (left) The scene at Snowdon Summit (3,493ft up) with No 3 *Wyddfa*, of 1895, approaching and No 6 *Padarn*, of 1922, waiting to leave for Llanberis. (above) Morning activity at Llanberis shed on 1 June 1978. No 4 *Snowdon* leaves with a train for the Summit while No 5 *Moel Siabod* (nearest) and No 7 *Aylwin* are on shed./*Both: Brian Morrison*

SMR Miscellany (above) An August 1953 scene at Hebron with No 7 *Aylwin* (left) on one of the line's nine coaches in its original open state with curtains and (right) No 5 *Moel Siabod* with the works bogie car. (below) Llanberis on 7 April 1976 when snow and ice prevented working beyond Clogwyn. No 7 on shed, No 4 arriving on a pw special – note the modifications to the works car and the line's sole wagon. (above centre) Works plates of No 4 *Snowdon* and (above right) her nameplate and Hunslet rebuilding plate. (bottom right) No 6 *Padarn* on its way up to Snowdon, near Hebron./H. C. Casserley; R. E. Ruffell; T. J. Edgington (two); Brian Morrison

The 2ft 6in gauge Welshpool & Llanfair Light Railway was open for general goods traffic 1903-56 and for passengers 1903-31. Almost exactly 60 years after the original opening, the W&LLRP Co Ltd restarted passenger services on 6 April 1963.

These views illustrate earlier days. (above) A Welshpool-bound freight at Cyfronydd on 24 August 1948. (top right) *The Earl*, one of the line's two original 0-6-0Ts, by now GWR No 822, enters Llanfair Caereinion with a passenger train, in the last year of passenger working. Note yard crane (right). (right) Llanfair on 24 August 1948./*LPC. H. C. Casserley;*

Right: When the last train ran on the Welshpool & Llanfair on 3 November 1956 (an enthusiasts' special), moves had already been made to set up a preservation society. Happily, British Railways did not attempt to dismantle the line, or to scrap rolling stock. Of the locomotives, No 822 *The Earl* (left) went to Oswestry Works for repair in March 1956 but did not return to the Railway. No 823 *Countess* stayed at Welshpool shed after the 1956 closure but joined the 'gentleman' at Oswestry Works in May 1958, where both are seen in store on 14 August of that year./*Brian Morrison*

The earlier days of W&LLR preservation. (top left) The Railway will never again run right through Welshpool but this was possible back in 1963. *The Countess* is flagged across Church Street, Welshpool, on 6 April 1963 on returning from the opening ceremony at Llanfair. (left) The interior of one of the coaches obtained from the Zillertalbahn, Austria, in its first season in Wales. (above) A view across ripening barley of *The Earl* and three Austrian coaches near Castle Caereinion with the 16.15 from Llanfair on 18 August 1971./*P. F. Winding; T. J. Edgington; G. F. Gillham*

Welshpool & Llanfair, immigrant and native. (above) The ex-German Military Railways 0-8-0T, obtained from the Styrian Government Railways, Austria, in 1969, latterly No 699.01, now No 10 *Sir Drefaldwyn*.

No 10 nears Llanfair alongside the River Banwy on 30 April 1972. (right) *The Earl* waits at Castle Caereinion with a goods train during the Open Weekend of 14 May 1978./*David Eatwell; R. E. B. Siviter*

More W&L immigrants. (left) The impressive ex-Bowaters modified Meyer-type 0-4-4-0T *Monarch*, the last new narrow gauge steam engine to be built for UK commercial service. She arrived at Llanfair in 1966 and is now No 6. She drifts through the quiet scenery between Sylfaen and Castle Caereinion, Llanfair-bound, on an evening train on 3 June 1978. (bottom left) *Monarch* arrives at Llanfair with the same train, on the same day. (below) From a sugar mill in Antigua came Kerr, Stuart-built 0-6-2T *Joan*, W&L No 12, with (left) 0-6-0 ex-Naval diesel *Chattenden*, both seen at Llanfair in June 1978. /All: Brian Morrison

Left: Isle of Man Railway. In 1905 the Isle of Man Railway absorbed the island's two smaller companies, the Manx Northern and the Foxdale Railway, both of 3ft gauge. Douglas shed in the early days of this century with what appears to be 2-4-0T No 8 *Fenella.*/*LPC*

Below left: One of the most substantial survivors of Manx Northern equipment in recent years has been the Dubs-built 0-6-0T of 1885, *Caledonia,* IoMR No 15, built for freight working to Ramsey Harbour. It is seen here at Douglas in August 1971./*Keith Smith*

Sparse and abundant passenger patronage on the Isle of Man Railway. (right) The Foxdale branch train in July 1933, in the rather bleak country of that area, behind No 6 *Peveril.* (below) Kirk Braddan station on the Peel line was noted for the out and back working on Sundays for the open air church service nearby. A July 1933 scene. /*Both: H. C. Casserley*

Left: The little ¾-mile long 2ft gauge Groudle Glen railway was built purely for tourists and opened in 1896. In decline by the late 1950s, it reopened in 1961 for two seasons only and this attractive scene of *Polar Bear*, a Bagnall 2-4-0T of 1906, was taken in 1961./*Ian Allan Library*

The old Isle of Man Railway ceased its public carrier rail services – passenger, goods and parcels – in November 1965. From 1967-71 it was leased to a private group and for 1967/8 services were operated on all lines. Two scenes from that period: (above) Douglas station with the 10.20 departure on 19 June 1968, No 10 *G H Wood* leading with 4 coaches for Peel and 4 coaches, 1 wagon and 1 van for Ramsey, the train to be divided at St Johns. No 12 is assisting at the rear. (below) The picturesque Ramsey line with a train on Glen Wyllin viaduct./*G. D. King; J. Spencer Gilks*

The Manx Electric Railway (3ft gauge) from Douglas to Ramsey, and the Snaefell Mountain Railway (3ft 6in gauge) are two other reasons for visiting the Isle of Man. (above) Approaching Derby Castle terminus — MER motor car No 21 in the green and white livery carried by some cars in the late 1950s/early 1960s, with cross-bench trailer and van in tow in July 1959. (below) Typical scene, above old Laxey, with cross-bench motor-car and trailer bound for Douglas in July 1959. (top right) The MER had a contract until 1975 to carry mail, which is being unloaded at Douglas in March 1969. Winter services ended in 1975. (bottom right) Snaefell car No 1 at Laxey; roof boards now removed./*Frank Church (two); A. R. Taylor; P. J. Sharpe*

Right: Victorian evening at Douglas station in the 1960s./*M. Dunnett*

Latterly only the Douglas-Port Erin line of the Steam Railway has operated, and the line was formally nationalised on 13 January 1978. (below) Santon embankment is traversed by No 4 *Loch* with the 10.15 from Port Erin on 5 July 1971. (below right) *Loch* arrives at Port Erin on 28 May 1978 with a train from Douglas./*G. D. King; Ray Dauwalder*

(Left) *Loch,* again, with cylinder cocks blowing, shunts in Douglas yard. (above) Reflections at Silver Burn bridge, Castletown, as a Port Erin train crosses at Easter 1971./*Both: A. Stevenson*

New purpose for the narrow gauge

Narrow gauge railways of a practical if horse- or man-powered type existed to carry slate in North Wales from the very start of the 19th century. This was not coincidental, for it was only in the last quarter of the 18th century that the slate industry developed. The success and example of the Festiniog Railway in developing an efficient narrow gauge railway and, later, in the 1860s in demonstrating the practicability of steam power on less than 2ft gauge, is an already well documented story. But what is surprising is that the less than standard gauge made so little progress until the last quarter of the 19th century. Indeed, the first *English* narrow gauge line was the original 3ft Ravenglass & Eskdale, vintage 1875. True, some industrial lines were older than this: Rosling Bennett describes a small 0-4-0ST of a gauge variable from 2ft 3in-3ft which had worked in the Delamere Forest from 1862.

Given the universality of steam power, the comparative lack of interest in a less than standard gauge railway of whatever kind is perhaps intriguing. Nonetheless, there were a few experiments with smaller and miniature gauge locomotives designed to explore the practicability of steam. But, as Clayton, Jacot and Butterell so ably show in *Miniature Railways* (Vol 1) (Oakwood Press 1970), generally they were restricted to unpublicised pleasure lines in rich men's gardens.

A slight surprise – even perhaps a hint of Puritanism – usually accompanies mention of pleasure railways. If motor transport has derived much of its strength and popularity from the fact that people enjoy motoring, then we should not deny rail similar access to general appeal. Fortunately, in the past a few individuals have thought similarly and in creating small railways for pleasure-seekers they have also been concerned to demonstrate that their lines could also serve as limited freight carriers, or as providers of a public (or relatively public) passenger facility. Hence Sir Arthur Heywood's Duffield Bank Railway experimented with from 1877 on a 'minimum' (ie practicable) gauge of 15in; Sir Robert Walker's Sand Hutton Miniature and Light Railways (15in 1912-20 and 18in gauge from 1922-32); the conversion of the Ravenglass & Eskdale to 15in gauge in 1915 and Howey and Zborowski's Romney, Hythe & Dymchurch Railway of 1926. All these, at some time, aimed to do more than provide railways as entertainment. Notable also were the Blakesley Miniature Railway (1903); Miniature Railways Ltd's enterprises from 1904, and particularly their Rhyl Miniature Railway of 1911. The last named is still with us, as is the Fairbourne Railway, converted to 15in gauge in 1916, although the Rhyl railway was temporarily out of use until resuscitated in 1978.

But after the 1920s there was little development in this field, although a 10in line, the Surrey Borders & Camberley, appeared and died in the last year of interwar peacetime. Indeed, in the postwar period both Ravenglass and RH & DR had experienced crises which might have led to their demise in the early 1960s and early 1970s respectively. But then the revival of the small gauge railway began, fuelled by the growth in leisure activities, and aided by the explosion of private motoring. First, perhaps, was the Lincolnshire Coast Light Railway, then the Bicton Woodland Railway, and, with the closure of the North Wales slate quarry systems, suitable and picturesque small locomotives (of just less than 2ft gauge) became available. Meanwhile, other industrial railway equipment was resurrected for preservation and use during the 1960s: the former sand-carrying 2ft gauge railway that has been developed into the Leighton Buzzard Light Railway; and the survival of part of the Bowaters railway as the volunteer-operated Sittingbourne & Kemsley Light Railway. There have also been the successful and more commercially inspired 'stately homes and gardens' type of railways at Knebworth House, Bressingham, Whipsnade and Hollycombe. Following earlier examples, perhaps, narrow gauge has flourished on the trackbeds of defunct wider gauge lines. Along part of the 4ft Padarn Railway beside Llyn Padarn there is the Llanberis Lake Railway, opened in 1971 and, elsewhere in Wales, the Bala Lake Railway from Bala to Llanuwchllyn. On 2ft gauge the latter provides services on the path of the former GWR Ruabon-Dolgellau standard gauge line.

Behind the scenes, too, are further narrow gauge projects, even more ambitious. These can draw on almost limitless supplies around the world of equipment of varying histories and gauges, moribund or shortly to become redundant. Since there is no sign that the public is tired of railways as a form of entertainment, the enterprises of the past two decades may be but a curtain-raiser to greater narrow gauge surprises.

Below: Stately home narrow gauge. The 1¼-mile 1ft 11½in gauge Knebworth West Park and Winter Green Railway operated by Pleasure-Rail Ltd opened in 1971 as an attraction at Knebworth House, Herts. Ex-Penrhyn Railway quarry 0-4-0ST *Lilla,* **built Hunslet 1891, bustles along under the trees on 3 September 1978.**/*P. H. Groom*

Above: The Rhyl Marine Lake Miniature Railway (15in gauge) dates back to 1911 but was out of use from 1970 until revived in 1978. Original and locally built 4-4-2 *Michael*, of 1920, takes its passengers round the lake on opening day, 8 July./*Larry Goddard*

Right: Miniature railway on the Cambrian Coast. The Fairbourne Railway (also 15in gauge) was converted from a 2ft horse tramway in the middle of the first world war. (top right) *Count Louis* (of 1924) worked most of the Fairbourne trains in the interwar period and reposes at Fairbourne in July 1975. An example of a postwar miniature locomotive (bottom right), *Katie,* a Guest-built 2-4-2 of 1956./*Both: T. J. Edgington*

The Ravenglass & Eskdale Railway, of 2ft 9in gauge, survived from 1875-1912 and was reopened in stages as a 15in gauge line between 1915-17. (above) In its old guise, as a 2ft 9in gauge line with Manning Wardle 0-6-0T *Devon* at Eskdale. (below) The imaginative but ungainly 4-6-0 + 0-6-4 articulated locomotive named *River Mite,* produced by the R&ER from two 'scale model' 4-6-2s in 1928, which lasted only for nine years./*The late W. H. Whitworth*

Top: *River Irt,* an 0-8-2, was rebuilt by the R&ER in 1927 from Sir Arthur Heywood's Duffield Bank locomotive *Muriel* of 1894. She is seen here in pre-1972 condition on 1 August 1967 at Ravenglass. */T. J. Edgington*

Above: The handsome 2-8-2 *River Esk,* of the R&ER, dates from 1923 and is seen nearly fifty years later on 30 May 1972. The train is traversing Gilbert's Cutting – a 400ft diversion opened in March 1964 to obviate sharp reverse curves west of Beckfoot./*T. J. Edgington*

An interesting comparison of latter-day Ravenglass locomotive practice. (right) *Northern Rock,* a powerful 2-6-2 built at Ravenglass in 1976, makes a fine picture as it passes between Muncaster Mill and the River Mite with its nose to the stable door on the last train of the day from Dalegarth (Eskdale [Dalegarth] from 1979) on 26 March 1978. (below) The 0-8-2 *River Irt* was rebuilt in 1972 and received new boiler mountings altering her scale model appearance (as seen on p105). She is seen at Irton Road in May 1972, as first rebuilt. In 1966 Clarkson's of York built the 2-8-2 *River Mite* to scale model proportions, an updated sister to *River Esk.* Caught (bottom right) as she passed *River Irt* at Irton Road in April 1979. Note the current appearance of *Irt* and her air brake pump.
/ *David Eatwell; T. J. Edgington; R. E. Ruffell*

The 15 inch Romney, Hythe & Dymchurch, built 1926 and opened to traffic in July 1927, relies on a fine stud of 4-6-2s and two 4-8-2s. Their size can be deceptive given their almost exact scale. No 3 *Southern Maid* (above) at speed with the non-stop 'Golden Jubilee' Dungeness-Hythe near St Mary's Bay on 17 August 1978. (below) 'Brother' engine No 2 *Northern Chief* in 1976./*P. H. Groom; Brian Morrison.*

Contrasts in scale: (top right) Lade road overbridge at the western end of the line dwarfs Pacific *Southern Maid* bound for Dungeness on 22 June 1977. (bottom right) Viewed from Dungeness lighthouse the bleak landscape overwhelms Canadian-style Pacific No 9 *Winston Churchill* as it arrives at the station on 13 June 1976./*Both: David Eatwell*

Four contrasting types of RH&DR motive power. (top left) Pacific *Northern Chief* at the eastern terminus, Hythe, on 15 August 1976. (bottom left) 4-8-2 No 6 *Samson* at New Romney on 15 August 1976, ready to leave for Hythe. (above) Canadian outline No 10 *Doctor Syn* in 1976 on New Romney turntable (acquired from the Lynton & Barnstaple Railway on closure). (below) The RH & DR acquired Krupp-built 4-6-2 *Black Prince* in May 1976. The driver awaits the 'right-away' at Hythe on 17 August 1978./*Brian Morrison (three); P. H. Groom*

The 18in gauge Bicton Woodland Railway, near Budleigh Salterton, Devon, was constructed in 1962 and used some equipment from the Royal Arsenal Railway, Woolwich, It opened on 6 April 1963. (top left) This is Bicton station on 7 July 1964 with No 1 *Woolwich,* an oil-fired 0-4-0T built by Avonside in 1916. Left is the small Ruston diesel 0-4-0 *Bicton.* (bottom left) The striking articulated 0-4-4-0 diesel No 3 *Carnegie,* built by Hunslet in 1954, at Bicton in July 1977./*T. J. Edgington; Brian Morrison*

Above: The Leighton Buzzard Light Railway was built in 1919, to 2ft gauge, to move sand from pits in the area. By 1969 through traffic had ceased but two years earlier enthusiasts had taken over part of the line for weekend operations and by the next season the railway was firmly established as the Leighton Buzzard Narrow Gauge Railway. Motive power has come from many sources such as No 1 *Chaloner,* a de Winton vertical boiler 0-4-0T built in 1877 and used in North Wales slate quarries./*T. J. Edgington*

Leighton Buzzard Narrow Gauge Railway motive power review. (top left) In its centenary year *Chaloner,* following a major overhaul, heads for the terminus, Page's Park, on 16 July 1977. (bottom left) No 2 *Pixie,* built Kerr, Stuart 1922, spent most of her life at a roadstone quarry, coming to the LBNGR in 1968. No 2 coasts into Page's Park on 26 September 1971. (right) Orenstein & Koppel 0-4-0WT No 11 *P. C. Allen* came from Spain, and emerges through the trees at Marley's Bank in July 1971. (below) Line-up at Page's Park on 2 July 1977 with Baguley 1921-built 0-4-0T No 3 *Rishra,* an import from Calcutta, leading a wide range of typical internal combustion locomotives./*David Eatwell (two); P. H. Groom; Kevin Lane*

Left: Stately homes and gardens – 1 The Knebworth West Park and Winter Green Railway has run some successful steam weekends featuring locomotives visiting from other centres. This (above left) was the 'Wonderful World of Wheels' weekend of 2 September 1978 with resident No 1 (left), a 1922 Hunslet 0-4-0ST ex-Dinorwic and (right) 'Wren' class Kerr, Stuart 0-4-0ST No 9 *Peter Pan* on holiday from the Albany Steam Museum, Isle of Wight. (bottom left) Ex-East German (DR) 0-8-0 No 99.3461 was on loan to Knebworth for a while (but has now gone abroad) and is seen on 24 July 1976./*D. Trevor Rowe; David Eatwell*

Above: Stately homes and gardens – 2 Bressingham Gardens includes a 1ft 11½in gauge railway through the nurseries and woodland and one of the locomotives is *Bronwllyd,* basically the Hudswell Clarke 0-6-0WT No 1643 of 1930 (latterly at Penrhyn quarries) but given a new boiler at Bressingham. Owner Alan Bloom is driving in this July 1971 picture./*David Eatwell*

Right: Stately homes and gardens – 3 The Hollycombe Woodland Railway, at Hollycombe House, near Liphook, has a 2ft gauge line on which operates No 1 *Caledonia,* a Barclay 0-4-0WT of 1931 (formerly No 70 at Dinorwic) surrounded by mixed vegetation on 2 July 1978./*R. A. Cover*

We met the 2ft 6in gauge Bowaters railway earlier in this book and these two pages contrast past and present. (top) Kemsley Mill on 4 October 1969 with four locomotives still working on, or preserved on, the Sittingbourne & Kemsley Light Railway. (Left to right) *Premier*, and *Melior*, 0-4-2STs of 1905/24, *Unique*, the Bagnall fireless 2-4-0 of 1924 and 0-6-2T *Superb* of 1940. (above) Working hard in the last days of industrial operation, *Superb* heads the 15.20 to Kemsley Mill out of Ridham Dock on 4 October 1969, the date also of the above picture./*Both: D. A. Idle* (right) Present-day preservation: Bagnall 0-6-2T *Triumph* of 1934 sets out from Sittingbourne for the Kemsley Down terminus on 22 August 1970./*Dave Greenwood*

Above left: S&KLR 0-4-2ST *Premier* disposes of the stock of the last train of the day at Sittingbourne on 26 August 1974./*Brian Morrison*

Left and above: From the surrealist setting of Bowaterscape some of that operator's motive power went to the equally unlikely surroundings of Whipsnade Zoo, to work the Whipsnade and Umfolozi Railway. This now consists of a 3-mile circuit among rhinos and camels, the first section opening on 26 August 1970. (left) Kerr, Stuart 0-4-2ST *Excelsior* on 17 September 1978./*David Eatwell* (above) Kerr, Stuart 0-6-2T *Superior* on 28 August 1976. /*Brian Morrison*

Right: Larger motive power is being imported to Britain, too, such as David Shepherd's 1896-built Sharp, Stewart 4-8-0 No 390 (ex-Rhodesia Railways, ex-Zambezi Sawmills Railway), marooned on 3ft 6in track at Whipsnade, but able to be steamed as on 10 September 1976./*David Eatwell*

Top left: The electric narrow gauge: the 2ft 9in gauge Seaton and District Electric Tramway Company with a 2½-mile line. Activity at the Seaton terminus on 20 July 1977./*Brian Morrison*

Diesel narrow gauge: (bottom left) The Llanberis Lake Railway (see page 124) uses a Simplex 0-4-0 diesel, No 9 *Dolgarrog,* to work a refreshment 'coach' to the Cei Llydan picnic and leisure area alongside Llyn Padarn. (above) The three-mile 1ft 11½in gauge Bala Lake Railway opened on 13 August 1972, along part of the trackbed of the GWR Ruabon-Dolgelley line. Motive power includes this 1973 Severn Lamb diesel-hydraulic Bo-Bo No 4 *Meirionedd* attracting custom for Bala, at Llanuwchllyn, on 30 May 1978./*Both: Brian Morrison*

123

The Rheilffordd Llyn Llanberis (Llanberis Lake Railway) is a private venture, promoted partly as an enterprising means of employing former quarry workers in an area of high unemployment. Along the trackbed of the Padarn Railway (see page 34) there is now a 2-mile stretch of 1ft 11½ gauge railway, partly opened in the summer of 1971 and throughout in 1972. (top left) Trains cross at Cei Llydan on 28 May 1978: No 3 *Dolbadarn* (left) heading for the main terminus of Gilfach Ddu and No 1 *Elidir* bound for Penllyn. Both are Hunslet 0-4-0STs, ex-Dinorwic Quarries: *Dolbardan* dates from 1922, *Elidir* (originally *Red Damsel* and, earlier, *Enid*) from 1889. (bottom left) *Dolbadarn* coasts into Cei Llydan from Gilfach Ddu and (above) *Elidir* at Gilfach Ddu, taking water. /All: Brian Morrison

125

The Bala Lake Railway is a fitting tailpiece for this look at the new narrow gauge. (above) Bala station on 30 May 1978 with ex-Dinorwic quarry 1903-built Hunslet 0-4-0ST *Maid Marian* amid plenty of action. *Maid Marian* reached Bala by way of Bressingham and Llanberis (second time) and belongs to the Maid Marian Fund. (top right) Last vehicle in *Maid Marian's*

train is a new closed coach, a similar example of which was being built for the railway at Gwynedd Engineering Services Ltd, Bala, in May 1978.

Bottom right: The former GWR Llanuwchllyn standard gauge station dwarfs *Maid Marian* and her train, on arrival in May 1978./*All: Brian Morrison*

Above: Appropriate farewell from the father of preservation, the Talyllyn, with ex-Corris 0-4-2ST No 4 *Edward Thomas* **leaving Abergynolwyn on 2 June 1978.**/*Brian Morrison*